First World War
and Army of Occupation
War Diary
France, Belgium and Germany

14 DIVISION
41 Infantry Brigade
London Regiment
33rd (City of London) Battalion
7 June 1918 - 31 May 1919

WO95/1895/4

The Naval & Military Press Ltd
www.nmarchive.com
Published in association with The National Archives

Published by

The Naval & Military Press Ltd

Unit 10 Ridgewood Industrial Park,

Uckfield, East Sussex,

TN22 5QE England

Tel: +44 (0) 1825 749494

www.naval-military-press.com

www.nmarchive.com

This diary has been reprinted in facsimile from the original. Any imperfections are inevitably reproduced and the quality may fall short of modern type and cartographic standards.

© Crown Copyright
Images reproduced by permission of The National Archives, London, England, 2015.

Contents

Document type	Place/Title	Date From	Date To
Heading	WO95/1895-4		
Heading	14th Division 41st Infy Bde 33rd Bn London Regt (R.B) Jun 1918-May 1919 From U.K.		
Heading	War Diary of 33rd Battn The London Regt (Rifle Bde) From 7-6-18 To 30-6-18 (Volume I)		
War Diary	Clacton-on-Sea	07/06/1918	16/06/1918
War Diary	Pirbright	18/06/1918	30/06/1918
Heading	War Diary of 33rd Bn The London Regt (Rifle Bde) From 1-7-18 To 31-7-18 (Volume II)		
War Diary	Pirbright	01/07/1918	02/07/1918
War Diary	Folkestone	03/07/1918	03/07/1918
War Diary	Boulogne	04/07/1918	04/07/1918
War Diary	Rety	05/07/1918	10/07/1918
War Diary	Alembon-Sanghem	11/07/1918	11/07/1918
War Diary	Nordausques	12/07/1918	12/07/1918
War Diary	Les Marais	13/07/1918	14/07/1918
War Diary	St. Sylvestre Cappel	15/07/1918	29/07/1918
War Diary	Les Six Rues	30/07/1918	30/07/1918
War Diary	Tattinghem	31/07/1918	31/07/1918
Heading	War Diary of 33rd Bn The London Regt. (R.B) From 1-8-18 To 31-8-18 (Volume III)		
War Diary	Moulle	01/08/1918	20/08/1918
War Diary	St Jan De Biezen	21/08/1918	27/08/1918
War Diary	Brake Camp	28/08/1918	28/08/1918
War Diary	Ypres Front	28/08/1918	31/08/1918
Heading	War Diary of 33rd Battn The London Regt (Rifle Brigade) From 1/9/18 To 30/9/18 (Volume IV)		
War Diary	Ypres Front	01/09/1918	06/09/1918
War Diary	Brielen	07/09/1918	10/09/1918
War Diary	Brake Camp	11/09/1918	14/09/1918
War Diary	Ypres Front	14/09/1918	20/09/1918
War Diary	Steenvoorde	21/09/1918	26/09/1918
War Diary	Reninghelst	27/09/1918	28/09/1918
War Diary	Dickebush	28/09/1918	30/09/1918
Heading	War Diary of 33rd London Regt (Rifle Bde) From 1-10-18 To 31-10-18 (Volume IV)		
War Diary	Messines	01/10/1918	02/10/1918
War Diary	Comines Area	02/10/1918	16/10/1918
War Diary	Wulverghem	17/10/1918	17/10/1918
War Diary	Comines	18/10/1918	18/10/1918
War Diary	Roncq	19/10/1918	19/10/1918
War Diary	Herseaux	20/10/1918	31/10/1918
Miscellaneous	Report On Operations 12th To 15th Oct 1918	15/10/1918	15/10/1918
Heading	War Diary of 33rd Bn The London Regt (Rifle Brigade) From 1-11-18 To 30-11-18 (Volume V)		
War Diary	Helchin Front	01/11/1918	06/11/1918
War Diary	Dottignies	07/11/1918	08/11/1918
War Diary	Les Ballons	09/11/1918	14/11/1918
War Diary	Bondues Area	15/11/1918	21/11/1918
War Diary	Bondues	22/11/1918	30/11/1918

Type	Description	From	To
Operation(al) Order(s)	33rd Bn The London Regiment (Rifle Brigade) Operation Order No.30	04/11/1918	04/11/1918
Miscellaneous	Reference Sheet 29 S W	05/11/1918	05/11/1918
Miscellaneous	Reference Sheet 29 S W	06/11/1918	06/11/1918
Heading	War Diary of 33rd Bn London Regt (Rifle Bde) From 1-12-18 To 31-12-18 (Volume VI)		
War Diary	Bondues	01/12/1918	11/12/1918
War Diary	Marcq	12/12/1918	31/12/1918
Heading	War Diary of 33rd Bn The London Regt (Rifle Bde) From 1-1-19 To 31-1-19 (Volume VII)		
War Diary	Marcq	01/01/1919	03/01/1919
War Diary	Tourcoing	04/01/1919	31/01/1919
Heading	War Diary of 33rd Bn The London Regt (Rifle Bde) From 1-2-19 To 28-2-19 (Volume VIII)		
War Diary	Tourcoing	01/02/1919	28/02/1919
Heading	War Diary of 33rd Bn The London Regt (R B) From 1/3/19 To 31/3/19 (Volume IX)		
War Diary	Tourcoing	01/03/1919	29/03/1919
Heading	War Diary of 33rd Bn The London Regt (R B) Period 1-4-19 To 30-4-19 (Volume X)		
War Diary	Tourcoing	02/04/1919	19/04/1919
Heading	War Diary of 33rd Battn The London Regiment (Rifle Bde) From 1.5.19 To 31.5.19 (Volume XI)		
War Diary	Tourcoing	13/05/1919	31/05/1919

Woos/1895/2005 (4)

Woos/1895 (4)

14TH DIVISION
41ST INFY BDE

33RD BN LONDON REGT(R.B.)
JUN 1918 - MAY 1919

From UK

CONFIDENTIAL

WAR DIARY

OF

33rd BATTN. THE LONDON REGT (RIFLE BDE)

FROM 7-6-18   To. 30-6-18

May 19   (VOLUME I)

 10/20.   CAPT. & Adjt for Lt Col.

COMMDG. 33rd BATTN. THE LONDON REGT (RIFLE BDE)

FIELD.
27/7/18.

Army Form C. 2118.

WAR DIARY
or
INTELLIGENCE SUMMARY.
(Erase heading not required.)

Instructions regarding War Diaries and Intelligence Summaries are contained in F.S. Regs., Part II and the Staff Manual respectively. Title pages will be prepared in manuscript.

Place	Date	Hour	Summary of Events and Information	Remarks and references to Appendices
Clacton on Sea	7/6/18		The 33/105th (R.London Regt (R.F.) Bn. formed at Clacton on Sea a/w W.O. Letter 20/Inf/1117 (A.G. 2A) 1/6/18 and to be administered by O.C. 29th London Regt until Parker taken. Staff of 105 O.R's formed from 29th London Regt. 2/Lts W.D. CASS 3rd London, W.C. HANCOCK 21st London Regt and Lt K. HARE 25th London joined the Bn.	p. 2/3
"	8/6/18		2/Lt E.H. ROBINSON 3rd London and MAJOR C.E.B. COCKELL 32nd London Regt joined	p. 2/3
"	9/6/18		Lt N.G.F. ROBSON 2/7th Devon Regt and Hon. Lt & Q.M. T. MIDDLETON joined.	p. 3/3
"	10/6/18		Draft of 160 O.R. from 17th Gloucesters and 244 from 28th Sentinel Light Infantry joined during period 10/6/18.	p. 2/3
"	11/6/18		Draft of 86 O.R. from 2/8th Essex Regiment.	p. 2/3
"	12/6/18		Capt. W.H. ROPER joined from 3rd East Yorks and appointed Adjutant. Lt. C.V. MAIDMENT, 9th London joined, also 2/Lt C. MEADOWCROFT, S.H. STILES, E.S.R. SPERLING and J.D.E. MILLER from 17th Beds/Herts. Draft of 86 O.R. from 2/7th Devons, 82 O.R. from 2/10th Devigs yeo and 194 O.R. from 30th London joined.	p. 2/3
"	13/6/18		Lt. Col. STACPOOLE J.W. R. Munster Fusiliers joined and assumed Command. J.R. Battalion 2/Lt R.L. CHARLTON, 19th Londons, Capt. C.B. McCLURE, 9th Londons and Lt. J.G. OSBORNE also 2/Lt H. GODDARD. 3rd Essex joined.	p. 2/3
"	14/6/18		Capt. A.E. FRENCH 6th London Regt, Capt. J.R. PYPER M.C., Capt. J.R. PYPER M.C. 3rd Londons, Lt. W.J. PALK M.C. 3rd East Surrey 2/Lts E.D. VINSON, R. NITTINGHAM, S.H.K. GELLER 3rd R. Sussex Regt. R. BAXTER Leicest. Kent Cyclist and W.G. Cayzer 18th London joined.	p. 2/3
"	15/6/18		Draft of 150 O.R. from 14th Londons, 16 from 22nd Londons, 14 from 30th Londons and 4 from 21st Londons joined.	

Major S.M. Boyle McGrath Rifles A/O.C. 33rd London Regt Rifles

Army Form C. 2118.

WAR DIARY
or
INTELLIGENCE SUMMARY.
(Erase heading not required.)

(2)

Place	Date	Hour	Summary of Events and Information	Remarks and references to Appendices
Clacton-on-Sea	16.6.18		19 O.R. from 23rd (R) Bau. Regt. R.C. joined.	h. J.B
			Major J.C.B. Boswell 3rd K.S.L.I. joined.	9. J.B
Pirbright	18.6.18		Battalion moved by rail to Bullswater Camp and were joined by the Training Cadre of 9/7th Batt.	9. J.B
			The Rifle Bde. who arrived from France to constitute the Battalion.	
			Lt. Col. Hon. M.T. Boscawen D.S.O. M.C., Capts. S.H. Shoveller M.C., C.A.M. Van Millingen M.C. J.C.B. Gray,	9. J.B
			A.E.H. Robinson D.S.O. & S. James M.C., 2/Lts. C.A. Johns M.C. and L. Morcom and Hon. Capt. & Q.M.	
			A. Coombs together with 44 O.R. comprising Training Staff.	9. J.B
	19.6.18		Battn. moved from Bullswater Camp to Stoney Castle Camp.	
			Lt. Col. J.W. Stackpoole resigned R. Mammets Position.	
			Batthen's resignation attached to "33rd London Regt (Rifle Brigade). Authority W.O. Letter No 20/Ly/1117	9. J.B
			(A.G. 2a) 18/6/18.	
	23.6.18		Major C.E.B. Cockell rejoined 2.26 H Miccoel Bell.	9. J.B
	24.6.18		Battn. Medical Inspection passed.	9. J.B
	26.6.18		All ranks who had not previously been vaccinated were so.	9. J.B
	27.6.18		Inspection by G.O.C. Musketry in afternoon.	9. J.B
			Lt. W.A. Williams, 2/Lt. H.E. Davies, E.E. Tinsley, H.S. Elborn, E. Badcock, C.S. Davis, W.B. Marsh,	
			and L. Gladding joined from 19th London.	
	29.6.18		Route march & musketry.	9. J.B
			2/Lts. E.E. Tinsley, L. Gladding & H.E. Davies rejoined 19th London.	
			2/Lt. R.C. Pickering 2/10th Leicester Regt joined for duty as Signalling Officer.	
	30.6.18		Musketry.	9. J.B
			141 O.R. Classified as Unfit by T.M.B. Transferred to 226th Musical Batt.	
			Lt. K. Marrs & 2/Lt. A. Nottingham & S.H.K. Geller also posted to 33 Graham Lycesbury.	

M.T. Boscawen
Comdg. 33 /3rd The London Regt (Rifle Bde)
Lt.Col.

CONFIDENTIAL

WAR DIARY

OF

33rd Bn. THE LONDON REGT (RIFLE BDE)

FROM 1-7-18   TO 31-7-18

(VOLUME II)

W.H. Roper Capt. a/ ... Lt Col

Commdg. 33rd Bn. THE LONDON Regt (RB)

1-8-18.

WAR DIARY
INTELLIGENCE SUMMARY.

(Erase heading not required.)

Army Form C. 2118.

Instructions regarding War Diaries and Intelligence Summaries are contained in F.S. Regs., Part II. and the Staff Manual respectively. Title pages will be prepared in manuscript.

(2)

Place	Date	Hour	Summary of Events and Information	Remarks and references to Appendices
PIRBRIGHT	1.7.18		Preparations for Embarkation overseas.	B
do	2.7.18	10 p.m. 11 p.m.	Entrained in two parties at BROOKWOOD for FOLKESTONE, where Battn billets for the night.	B
FOLKESTONE	3.7.18	9.30 a.m. 1 p.m.	Embarked for BOULOGNE, in two parties, & camped at OSTROHOVE overnight.	B
BOULOGNE	4.7.18		Entrained at GARE CENTRAL for MARQUISE; thence by march route to RETY.	B
RETY	5.7.18 to 9.7.18		Battalion training under C.O.'s management. Special attention being paid to Gas training, discipline and musketry. Specialist training also carried out.	B
-do-	10.7.18		Battalion marched to ALEMBON - SANGHEM area and billeted overnight.	B
ALEMBON-SANGHEM.	11.7.18		Battn marched to NORDASQUES and billets overnight.	B
NORDASQUES	12.7.18		Battn marched to LES MARAIS and billeted in immediate vicinity	B
LES MARAIS	13.7.18		Baths and inspections.	B
-do-	14.7.18		Battn entrussed and proceeded to ST. SYLVESTRE CAPPEL area.	B
ST. SYLVESTRE CAPPEL.	15.7.18 to 28.7.18		The Battn were engaged in improving the WINNEZEELE LINE. Battn drew and pitched tents. Each Coy. in turn, left off working party for two days cooking huters. Also one platoon for general training. Coy. Lewis Gunners for instruction and day on completion of work. In addition, Battalion carried out Lewis Gunnery, one hour's training. Draft of 67 O.R. joined on 18th inst.	B
-do-	29.7.18		Battn marched to LES SIX RUES area and billets overnight. Relieved by 29th D.L.I.	B
LES SIX RUES	30.7.18		Battn marched to TATTINGHEM and billets overnight	B
TATTINGHEM	31.7.18		Battn marched to MOULLE and billeted in village. Took over billets vacated by 29th L.I. Baths and general clean up.	B

M.J. Boscawen
Lt. Col.
Comdg. 33rd Bn. The London Regt. (The Rifle Bde)

CONFIDENTIAL

WAR DIARY

OF

33rd Bn THE LONDON REGT (R.B)

FROM 1-8-18   TO 31-8-18

(VOLUME III

W.H. Roper Capt. a/ Lt Col

Commdg 33rd LONDON REGT (R.B)

1-9-18.

WAR DIARY
or
INTELLIGENCE SUMMARY

(Erase heading not required.)

Army Form C. 2118.

Place	Date 1918	Hour	Summary of Events and Information	Remarks and references to Appendices
MOULLE	Aug 1/4th		Training. Company and Platoon drill, Musketry, Gas drill and specialist training.	B
-do-	5th	10 a.m.	Divisional Horse Show. Battn. obtained second place in aggregate points to 18th K.R.R Regt.	B
-do-	6/10th		Training. Musketry, Gas Drill, field firing, trench reliefs, extended order drill, advance on counter attack and consolidation of strong points, and specialist training	B
-do-	9th		2/Lt. D.P. Fox joined	B
-do-	11th	11 a.m.	2/Lt Morton + 8 O.R. attended special Divine Service at TERDINGHAM. H.M. The King was present.	B
-do-	12/17th		Training. Musketry, Gas drill, field firing, Bombing & Rifle Grenade practice, Extended order drill, Artillery formation, Deployments, Advance and rearguards, Company in attack, Ceremonial drill, night operations (Trench Relief) and Specialist training.	B
-do-	12th		2/Lt. C.W.R. Shurlock joined	B
-do-	13th		2/Lt. E. Smith joined.	B
-do-	16th	2.30pm	G.O.C. inspected Transport.	B
-do-	18th		Divine Service	B
-do-	19th		Company Drill.	B
-do-	20th	5.45 am	Battn. moved to WATTEN by march route. Transport moved to PROVEN area by march route. Thence by rail to PROVEN and marched to ROAD CAMP (ST JAN DE BIEZEN)	B
ST JAN DE BIEZEN	21st		Company drill and inspection	B
-do-	22/24th		Training. Musketry, Gas Drill, field firing, Ceremonial Drill.	B
-do-	25th		Divine Service	B
-do-	26th		Company Drill and inspection	B
-do-	27th	6 p.m.	Battalion Entrained at LANCASTER CAMP for BRAKE CAMP (Sheet 28. A.30 C & D)	B
BRAKE CAMP	28th	9 a.m. 11 a.m.	The Commanding Officer saw Company Commanders relative to front to be taken over. Reconnaissance of front position by the Commanding Officer, Company Commanders & Specialist Officers.	B

Army Form C. 2118.

WAR DIARY
~~INTELLIGENCE~~ SUMMARY

(Erase heading not required.)

Instructions regarding War Diaries and Intelligence Summaries are contained in F. S. Regs., Part II. and the Staff Manual respectively. Title pages will be prepared in manuscript.

Place	Date 1918	Hour	Summary of Events and Information	Remarks and references to Appendices
BRAKE CAMP	Aug 28th	7.45pm	Sheet 28 The Battalion entrained at 9.6.a.7.3. detrained at GODERICH I1c.2.8. and proceeded to relieve the 1/5th A & S.H. in Right Sub Section (I.10.c.5.9 to I.16.a.55.95) Dispositions "D" Coy right front, "B" Coy left front, "A" Coy Support and "C" Coy reserve. Battn. HQ YPRES RAMPARTS. Relief at 10.0pm finished.	1/3
"	29	—	Situation very quiet. Work on ploughing of Lines held. Patrols sent out. Failed to encounter any enemy.	1/3
YPRES FRONT	28/29 29/30			
"	30/31		News having been received that the enemy were evacuating the KEMMEL area patrols were sent out to ascertain if enemy were still holding line about CAMBRIDGE RD- LEINSTER FARM. These positions were found to be still occupied by the enemy. There was a slight increase in enemy activity in artillery, M.G. Rifle fire and aircraft. He also appeared to be very alert.	B

M. T. Murun
Commandant

3rd Bn. The London Regt. (The Rifle Bde)

CONFIDENTIAL

WAR DIARY

OF

33rd Batt. THE LONDON REGT (RIFLE BRIGADE)

From 1/9/18   To 30/9/18

(VOLUME IV.

W.H. Pope, Capt a/ Lt Col

30/9/18   Commdg 33rd Bn The London Regt (Rifle Bde)

Army Form C.

WAR DIARY
INTELLIGENCE SUMMARY.
(Erase heading not required.)

Instructions regarding War Diaries and Intelligence Summaries are contained in F.S. Regs., Part II. and the Staff Manual respectively. Title pages will be prepared in manuscript.

(6)

Place	Date 1918	Hour	Summary of Events and Information	Remarks and references to Appendices
YPRES FRONT.	Sept 1st/4th		Sheet 28. YPRES. Situation very quiet. Our patrols active. Working parties nightly under R.E. for improvement of trenches, erection of Battle Headquarters and wiring.	D
-do-	5th/6th		The Battalion was relieved on the night 5/6th by 16th/18th Manchester Regt, and on relief proceeded to Divisional Reserve in BROWN LINE near BRIELEN.	"
BRIELEN	7th/8th		The Battalion was engaged in repairing of Stopper Trench, erection of bomb stores, and digging buried cable French in vicinity of BROWN LINE.	"
-do-	9th/10th		The Battalion was relieved by 9th/10th H.L.I. on night of 9th/10th and moved to BRAKE CAMP. A30 Central.	"
BRAKE CAMP	11th/12th		Engaged in work as on 7th/8th.	"
-do-	13th/14th		The Battalion relieved the 6th Wilts Regt in Brigade Reserve on night 13th/14th. Disposition of Coys. Right "C" Centre "D" Left "B" Reserve "A".	"
YPRES FRONT.	14th/15th		Work under R.E. in Battle Area.	"
-do-	15th		"A" Coy moved to LILLE GATE and took over YPRES Defences from 10th H.L.I. "B" Coy moved to MENIN GATE and took over YPRES Defences from 10th H.L.I.	"
-do-	16th/18th		Work under supervision of R.E's in Battle area.	"
-do-	19th/20th		The Battalion was relieved by 2nd S.W. Borderers and 7th Seaforth Highlanders and entrained for STEENVOORDE area.	"
STEENVOORDE	21st/24th		Company training. Night attacks.	"
-do-	25th/26th		Battalion entrained for RENINGHELST.	"
RENINGHELST	27th/28th		The Battalion marched from RENINGHELST at 1 a.m. on 27th to vicinity of DICKEBUSH LAKE in Divisional Reserve for operations T 32.	"
DICKEBUSH	28th	4pm	"A" Coy moved to Spoil Bank and came under orders of G.O.C. 43rd Inf. Bde.	"
-do-	29th		"A" Coy moved to SPOIL BANK and was attached to 10th H.L.I.	"
-do-	29th/30th		Battalion returned to RENINGHELST.	"

Ph. W. Manro Lt. Col.
Commdg 32nd (orton Regt (R.K. B.A.)

CONFIDENTAL.

WAR DIARY OF

33rd LONDON REGT (RIFLE BDE)

FROM. 1-10-18   TO 31-10-18

(VOLUME IV)

[signature] Major
Commdg 33rd London Regt (Rifle Bde)

31/10/18.

Army Form C. 2118.

Instructions regarding War Diaries and Intelligence Summaries are contained in F. S. Regs., Part II. and the Staff Manual respectively. Title pages will be prepared in manuscript.

WAR DIARY
or
INTELLIGENCE SUMMARY
(Erase heading not required.)

(7)

Place	Date 1918 Oct	Hour	Summary of Events and Information	Remarks and references to Appendices
MESSINES	1/2d		Batln. moved by march route to MESSINES area in vicinity of J.0.23.b relieved the 1st London Regt (C.S. Rifles) on support. Disposition of Coys. Centre "B" Centre "C". Lt. Forwd "D". Rt. Rear "A". Lt Rear (in Cadre) "D".	Appx
COMINES AREA	2nd/3rd		Considerable patrolling took place to ascertain enemy's strength over crossing of Bridge.	Appx
	4th/5th		Batln. relieved the 23rd Bn. London Regt. on the night of 4/5th. Disposition of Coys - Left "D" Centre "C" Right "B" Reserve "A".	Appx
	5th		Lt.Col. M.T. Beauman D.S.O. M.C. proceeded on Special Leave. Major J.G.B. Brooke took over command of the Battn.	Appx
	6/7/th		Killed O.R.1. A/Lieut J. Munro O.R.1. Patrols pushed out to ascertain enemy's positions etc	Appx
	8/9/th		Battn. organised in the principles of storm ?? and ?? with a view of advance. infantry	Appx
	10/11/th		Battn. relieved by 29th A.I.F. operation previously conspired by ?? and taken over	Appx
	11th		Killed O.R.1.	Appx
	12th		Major J.G.B. Brooke evacuated. Major C.A.M. Van Straubenzee assumed Company Command.	Appx
	12/13/th		Battn. relieved 18th Yorks ?? in the right sub-sector of H.Q. Lower Bte. posts. Disposition of Coys. Rt front "D" Centre front "B". Left front "C" Support "A".	Appx
	13th		Major J. McLaren-Greig (18th Royal Scots) new Commander of the Battn.	Appx
	13th/14th		?? relief of night of 13/14th. The morning 15th Patrols extended enemy retreating because of R.I.F'S. Enemy pickets located & Secure on all areas of area.	Appx
	15th		At 05.30 hrs the operation ordered commenced in the Frontage of Division L/S being Joined ?? Sqm. Full report attached. Appendix 7a. Batln relieved by 14th Bn Argyll Sutherland Highlanders & relieved by Reliev.	Appx

Army Form C. 2118

WAR DIARY
or
INTELLIGENCE SUMMARY.
(Erase heading not required.)

Instructions regarding War Diaries and Intelligence Summaries are contained in F.S. Regs., Part II. and the Staff Manual respectively. Title pages will be prepared in manuscript.

Place	Date	Hour	Summary of Events and Information	Remarks and references to Appendices
WULVERGHEM	17th		Battn. engaged in general clean up.	
COMINES	18th		Battn. moved by lorries to area S. of COMINES & billeted overnight.	
TONCQ	19th		Battn. moved by march route to TONCQ & billets overnight.	
HERSEAUX	20th		Battn. continued the march to LUINGNE - HERSEAUX area. Billeted in HERSEAUX.	
"	21st		General clean up & inspections.	
"	22/26		Training - Musketry. Movements in gas attacks zones, various Drills.	
"	28th		L.O.C. Reb. inspected Battn. at Training.	
"	27th		Divine Service. B.C.C. C/Officer HERSEAUX.	
"	28/30th		Training - various lectures - Musketry, Range practice.	
"	31st		Battn. relieved the 1st H.R. Regt. & Sutherland Highlanders in the left sub-sector G.H.Q. Bizancourt.	

J.M. Clark Lt.
Comdg. 38th Bn. Canadian Inf. (Rifle Bn.)

COPY/

APPENDIX 7a.

REPORT ON OPERATIONS
12th to 15th Oct. 1918.

33RD. LONDON REGIMENT (RIFLE BRIGADE).

Ref, Sheet 28 S.E. 1/20.000.

1. On the night 12/13th. the Battalion was relieved the 18th. Bn. York and Lancaster Regt. in the right subsector held by the 41st. Inf. Bde.

2. From the time of this relief until the commencement of operations on the morning of the 15th October, considerable patrolling activity took place on both sides our forward posts pushing their way towards the line of the R.Lys and feeling the enemy's strength. During this period enemy Machine Guns and Trench Mortars were very active especially at night and his artillery shelled the forward and back areas fairly consistently, using gas shells freely.
On the night 14th/15th. October, no fewer than 4 enemy patrols strength varying from 6 to 10 were located and driven in on one side of the R.LYS.

3. On the morning of October 15th. at 0530 the operations which culminated in the passage of the LYS being forced, began.
Two Companies, "D" on the right and "C" on the left went forward to positions at which bridges were to be thrown across the R.LYS. "D" Company was under the command of Major C.A.M. Van Millingen, M.C. and "C" Company under the command of Captain J.R.PYPER, M.C. "B" Company under Lieut. Williams was in support and "A" Company under Capt. A.C.H.Robinson, D.S.O. was in reserve. At zero hour Battalion Headquarters had moved forward from ESPERANCE CABARET to Fme. de la BUSSCHE.
When our barrage at 0530 started on the enemy side of the R.LYS one Platoon from each of "D" and "C" Companies went forward covering R.E. parties carrying material for bridging. Work on No. 1 Bridge opposite BLANCHE FARM was begun immediately, the Lewis Gun section of No. 13 Platoon which kept down M.G. fire from enemy at BLANCHE Fme. By about 0630 the crossing was effected and the German post at BLANCHE Fme. consisting of 12 men under a Sergt. Major surrendered and their Machine Gun was captured and brought into use immediately.
No. 13 Platoon now pushed forward and opened fire in enemy elements in retreat. No. 15 Platoon crossed and threw out a defensive flank to the right and No. 14 on crossing moved eastwards against LAMLASH Fme. which was holding up the crossing of "C" Company.
At No. 2 Bridge more opposition was encountered and after material had been carried down, 2/Lt. Deverall, M.C. R.E. who was in charge of bridging operations and who throughout showed the greatest coolness and initiative suggested that for the moment a withdrawal was advisable. Several casualties had been caused and a number of the bridge floats had been punctured by M.G. fire. A Lewis Gun post was accordingly established at the old bridge and an orderly withdrawal to the copse 150x north of the River was carried out.
At about 0645 the Platoon from "D" Company was seen advancing towards LAMLASH FARM. No. 19 Platoon of "C" Coy. which had formerly gave forward again moved out and another attempt was made to throw the portable bridge across the river. Finally 2/Lt. Deverall, M.C. was successful in getting the demolished

– 2 –

CONFIDENTIAL

WAR DIARY

OF

33rd Bn THE LONDON REGT (RIFLE BRIGADE)

FROM 1-11-18   TO 30-11-18

(VOLUME V)

[signature] MAJOR
Commdg 33rd Bn LONDON REGT (RIFLE BDE)

30-11-18

Army Form C. 2118.

WAR DIARY
or
INTELLIGENCE SUMMARY.
(Erase heading not required.)

Instructions regarding War Diaries and Intelligence Summaries are contained in F. S. Regs., Part II. and the Staff Manual respectively. Title pages will be prepared in manuscript.

(a)

Place	Date	Hour	Summary of Events and Information	Remarks and references to Appendices
HELCHIN front.	P18 Nov 1/2		An Officer patrol crossed the ESCAUT with a view to ascertaining if Enemy post at C.5.b.45.50 was held and if not to occupy same. Heavy gas shelling caused fairly heavy gas casualties and a second patrol was sent to reinforce the first patrol. These patrols succeeded in crossing the river but on nearing the SLUICE were met by heavy machine gun and rifle fire. At 04.50 the patrols were withdrawn after having obtained very useful information.	N.C.f
- do -	2/3		An Officer patrol consisting of 1 officer and 14 other ranks was given orders to try and establish posts on the N. bank of the Sluice at C.5.a.3.4. The patrol succeeded in crossing the Sluice and established a LIASON post with the Y and L bombs on the left. The patrol thereupon moved along the E bank of the river to the Sluice gate without opposition. Upon crossing over the Sluice heavy M.G. fire was encountered at close range and several bombs were thrown. In accordance with instructions given the patrol returned leaving in position the LIASON post.	N.C.f
- do -	3/4		One platoon of "D" Coy was ordered to establish 3 posts on the EAST side of the River L'ESCAUT. The patrol crossed the bridge and established a post at C.S.a.0.4. The platoon was then split into two fighting patrols under Lt Osborn & 2/Lt Fuller respectively. One patrol rushed the Sluice Bridge and found same unoccupied by Enemy, but heavy wire. The patrol cut their way through wire and worked along the bank to assist the other patrol, which had, in the meantime, established themselves at Bridge where the Sluice runs into the marsh. Lt Osborn then took forward

WAR DIARY
or
INTELLIGENCE SUMMARY.
(Erase heading not required.)

Army Form C. 2118.

Place	Date 1918	Hour	Summary of Events and Information	Remarks and references to Appendices
HELCHIN front	Nov. 3/4		A Lewis Gun team and rifle section got into house at C.5.a.7.5. where the tending of a quantity of rifles and ammunition suggested that the Enemy had only just previously evacuated. Progress was reported to Batln. H.Q. and further instructions were received to establish posts at C.5.b.1.2. and C.5.b.3.6. The Lewis post was rushed and the Enemy were seen retiring as the patrol entered the house. The patrol then pushed forward to establish post at C.5.b.1.2. but were met with heavy M.G. fire at 50 yard range. Enemy fire was replied to by post established at C.5.b.3.6. and under cover of this the patrol withdrew, there being absolutely no cover of any kind.	
- do -	4/5	at 23.30	The Crossing of the River L'ESCAUT between U.30.c.40.45. and U.27.c.65.50. for the purpose of establishing posts along the E. side of the river was commenced. The operation was successful in every respect. Eleven posts were established, 23 prisoners and 3 machine guns captured, and severe casualties inflicted upon the Enemy. Casualties sustained during this operation 2 O.R. Killed 3 O.R. wounded. See APPENDIX 10A, 10B, & 10C. for detailed Operation Orders and report by Company Commander on action. The Battalion was relieved by 29th D.L.I. and on relief marched to DOTTIGNIES and billeted.	
do.	5/6			
DOTTIGNIES	7/8		General clean up, inspections and Company Drill.	
do	8		The Battalion was relieved by 20th Middlesex Regt. and marched to billets at LES BALLONS via CROMBION - MALCENSE - HERSEAUX	

WAR DIARY or INTELLIGENCE SUMMARY

Army Form C. 2118.

Place	Date	Hour	Summary of Events and Information	Remarks and references to Appendices
LES BALLONS	Nov 9th 1918		Training under Specialist Officers.	
do	10		Divine Service	
do	11		News received that ARMISTICE had been signed and that hostilities were to cease at 11.00. Band paraded through village playing national Airs. Troops notified of NEWS and training under Coy arrangements carried out.	
do	12		Inspection by Commanding Officer. Ceremonial Drill	
do	13		Route March and Ceremonial Drill	
do	14		Battalion moved by March route to BONDUES area. Torchlight party 10 Offrs & 40 O.R. proceeded to CROIX.	
BONDUES AREA	15		Arm drill closeorder drill and improvement to billets	
do	16		Ceremonial Drill - improvement of billets and recreational Training	
do	17		Divine Service	
do	18		Ceremonial Parade. Recreation and improvement of billets	
do	19		2 Officers 70 O.Rs formed into Agricultural party. B.G.C inspected Battalion. Recreation and improvement of billets	
do	20		Ceremonial Drill. Recreation & improvement of billets	
do	21		Rehearsal for Corps Commander's production inspection recreation & improvement of billets.	

T/Capt A/Major C.A.M. Van HILLINGEN and Capt. T.R. PYPER M.C. Awarded bar to Military Cross. Military Medal awarded to:- 860472 A/Cpl. G.T. BROADLEY, 860524 Pte. E. FORD, 860521 Pte. J.C. FREEMAN, 860607 Pte. T. OLIVER, 860689 Pte. T. WALKDEN and 2145 Pte. W. WISEMAN.

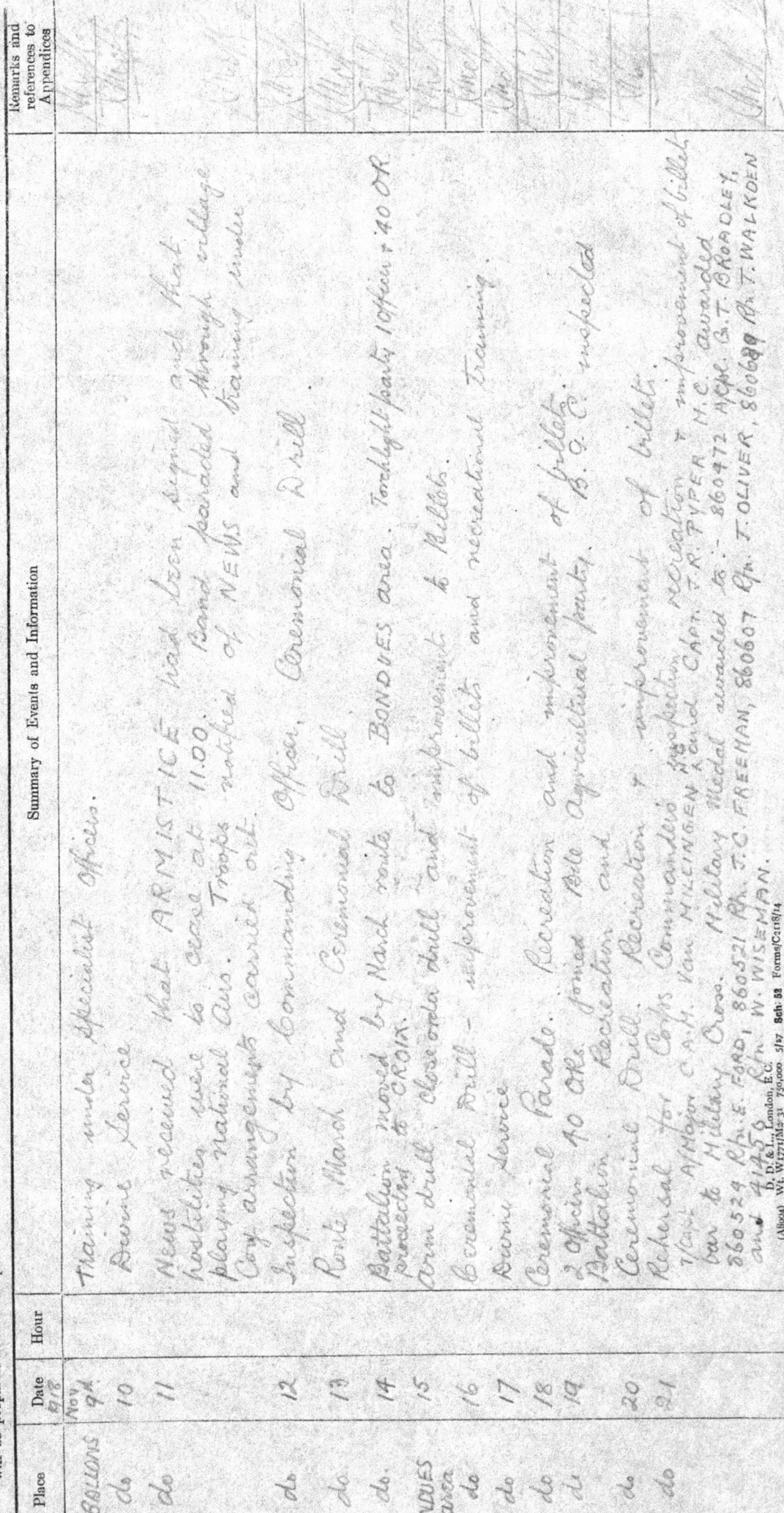

Army Form C. 2118.

WAR DIARY
or
INTELLIGENCE SUMMARY.
(Erase heading not required.)

(12)

Place	Date 1918	Hour	Summary of Events and Information	Remarks and references to Appendices
BONDUES	Nov 22		2/Lt H.W. SNODGRASS, C.L. WRIGHT, L.E. MARRIAN and H.R. PATSON joined R. & O. inspected Battalion Transport. Ceremonial Drill, recreation and improvement to billets.	
do	23		Coy training. Inspection of billets by Commanding Officer. Recreational Training.	
-do-	24		Divine Service	
-do-	25		Ceremonial Drill. Recreation and improvements to billets	
-do-	26		Refresher Corps Commander inspection ——— ditto ———	
-do-	27		Inspection of Brigade by XV Corps Commander. Recreation.	
-do-	28/30		Inspection of billets. Ceremonial parades. Coy training. Recreation and improvement of billets. During the later part of the month a number of the troops were given facilities for attending lectures at TOURCOING. The Education Section received close attention - though the actual commencement of classes on a general scale was not possibly owing to lack of suitable accommodation and materials requisite for the students. Military Medals awarded to 3860915 Mjr. T. KIRFOOT, 861115 Pte C. ROBINSON, 86H63 " T.A. HOTCHINS, 56H01 " F.T. ADAMS.	

30/11/18

M.E. [signature] Major
Commdg 33rd Lon. Regt. (Rifle Bde)

SECRET.   (10a)   Copy No........

33rd. Bn. The London Regiment (Rifle Brigade).

Operation Order No. 30.

1. The Battalion will move across the RIVER LESCAUT on left Company frontage tonight from U 30 c 40.45 to U 24 c 65.50.

This operation will be carried out by B and D Companies - B Company in Front supported by "D" Company.

The crossing will be effected by 3 bridges: No. 1 at U 30 c 40.45, No. 2 at U 30 c 80.85, No. 3 at U 24 b 65.50.

DISPOSITIONS: 1 Platoon of B Coy. to cross No. 1 Bridge.
                 1 "   " " " " "   "   No. 2   "
                 1 "   " " " " "   "   No. 3   "
                 1 "   " " " " " support at No. 1 Bridge.
                 1 "   " "D" " in support at No. 3 Bridge.

R.E.PARTIES. A Bridging Party of R.Es. will go forward at Zero with each of "B" Company crossing parties and throw over bridges at the 3 points under cover of infantry.

2. MOVEMENT AFTER CROSSING. Each crossing party will provide a post at their respective bridge-heads to act as covering parties, posts will be established along the E. side of the River at approx:

        U 30 c 4.1 ✻
        U 30 d 0.5
        U 30 b 0.2
        U 30 b 50.99
        U 24 d 80.50.
        U 24 b 85.25
        U 24 b 80.70 ✻

✻ These 2 must be established at the map reference given.
After establishing post No. 1 Party will work N to join No. 2 Party No. 2 Party will work N. to join with No. 3 Party and No. 3 Party will work S. to join with No. 2. Those working South will use a French Horn as a signal and those working North will use three blasts on a whistle as a signal.
The crossing will be covered by a preliminary bombardment of Artillery, 6" Stokes Mortar and M.Gs.
41st L.T.M.Bty. will co-operate under instructions to be detailed by O/C, 33rd. London Regt.
An Advance Dressing Station will be formed at "D" Coy's Headquarters.
Zero hour will be at 23.30.
All reports to be sent to Battalion Headquarters at U 22 c 10.85.

                         (SGD) G.B.McCLURE, Capt. & A/Adjt.
                         MEZI.

Dated 4/11/18.

COPY

T.B.

Reference Sheet 29 S.W.

C.A.P.

M.E.I.

(10 b)

Report on operations carried out on night [illegible] 5th/6th on front bounded by the line points U.30.c.4.5 and U.24.b.6.6.

The object of this operation was to establish line of posts east of LESBOEUFS [illegible] bridges made by R.E. after [illegible] covering parties while R.E. did the [illegible]

(a) U.30.c.4.5

(b) U.30.a.8.5

(c) U.24.b.6.6

Zero hour was at 2.30 after [illegible] of [illegible] duration had [illegible]. The R.E. [illegible] placed [illegible] the bridges [illegible] and [illegible] one platoon at each bridge.

Disposition of B. Coy.

No. 7 Platoon was detailed to cross the A Bridge [illegible] No. 5 Platoon the C Bridge.

(2)

No 6 Platoon was in support at 83 a 50 35.
The Platoon divided into No 1 and 3 Bridges
got over without much difficulty though
receiving considerable opposition on landing
on the far side. No 2 Bridge was
not successfully carried out at the
appointed time. Accordingly No 7
Platoon was ordered to join No 6's No 1 Bridge
which it succeeded in doing. Meantime
a few Sections of No 7 Platoon had
succeeded in getting across No 2 Bridge in
spite of the fact that it was not properly
secured and the water was lapping over to
a depth of 3'6" in the middle. These
sections pushed 100 yards south in the cover
of the bank and attacked the enemy's
& German positions from which we located
at 83 a d 17. In our order to work back
to bridgehead to establish post there and
then found that the R.E. had succeeded in
getting the bridge in working order.
No 7 Platoon moved up to take its position
as ordered after encountering heavy M.G.
fire from its left and considerable

(3)

opposition on his right.

No 7 Platoon which was now across L'ESCAUT and had turned left working along river bank towards position allotted to them. They encountered heavy machine gun opposition before they could find out one section was jettisoned. Our object was to be reached. The platoon who was to it soon ....

No 6 Platoon (support platoon) was now ordered to go forward over No 2 bridge and in 2nd echelon to No 5 & No 7 Platoons who were due to cross. This platoon encountered heavy mg fire and had difficulty in .... to it off ....

No 5 Platoon crossed the river at about No 10 where the bridge was across and met opposition from behind posts particularly on the right. A Lewis Gun team came to give a .... with a Grenadier EG. both sides the river bank after killing .... of the two ..... of this post the Lewis Gun was put out of action by a bullet through its barrel.

(5)

9   U 24 b 9 o
10   U 24 b 95 o

Company Headquarters was established at
S 29 b 50 15

Stretcher bearer posts were established at
the junction on the Yser bank

It seems that the enemy were
holding the position though not on by
the fact that fronts were pretty well together
but by the statement volunteered by a
prisoner that a whole company was
hidden in the direction of Potije.

We also found the enemy were shelling
somewhat heavily 200 yds in advance of
our established field. And also on river bank
they searched the side of the river bank
slightly. Our two platoons which were
at a 77 were ——————— our two platoons were
being relieved were to the southern side of
Grand Courte to form their new line
at ————

(Signed) E. B. G——
                        Capt
                E. B. Coy M & 21

10.45
a.m. 18

T.B.3 Copy1 (10 C) Reference Sheet 29.5.41

Adjt. MEZI

In continuation of my T.B.1 of yesterday's date, with regard to operations. The enemy shelled the left flank spasmodically from 06.00 until 12.00. This flank was quiet until 17.30 when slight shelling recommenced.

In front of No. 2 Bridge, however, and along the river bank the enemy shelled heavily with trench mortars, 5.9s, 4.2s and 77 mm. This was done with the evident intention of destroying the bridge and thereby cutting off communication. This lasted from about 15.00 to 15.30. This was coincident with shelling of the village of POTTES and OUERMIGES. All was quiet until 19.15, with the exception of trench mortar,

- 2 -

which carried on till 17.30.

At 19.15. a heavy enemy barrage on the same two sectors as above commenced, it being particularly strong around Bridge No. 3. At 20.00 this lifted on to main road running through U.24 A and C and N and N.W. of same.

LEFT FLANK. At 20.20 enemy machine guns with trench mortar support, worked forward from left flank, getting in rear of our left (No.10) post at U 24 b. 95.90. This post, however, putting up a strong fight, drove off the enemy party, consisting of 15 rank, who threw several bombs. Three or four of these were killed, and one wounded was left behind 5 yards in rear of former German post on River Bank. At 2000 reinforcements were asked for from D Coy. The runners however, being killed,

-3-

this party was delayed, and at 21.00 a Lewis Gun Team arrived. The enemy party had now been driven off and they were not needed, though they were taken across the river.
At 21.45 relief of 29th D.L.I. arrived.

CENTRE. Enemy M.G. party worked forward. This appeared to consist of 10 men. It does not appear that they attempted to reestablish post on River Bank.

SECTOR IN FRONT OF No. 2 BRIDGE.
At 17.15 an enemy party was seen in neighbourhood of POTTES Church, moving Southwards with evident intention of taking up position for counter attack. At the same time 2 men were seen in house at V.30.d.6.5 with a M.G. At 22.00 this party, 30 strong, crept to

- 4 -

within 30 yards of our post. I.E. about U.30.d.25.85 then attempting to work round right flank of bridgehead post and post at U.30.b.15.25. This party was driven off, leaving one man wounded and a few dead. The remainder managed to get back, taking with them several men who were slightly wounded. This party scattered considerably on its return journey. Very lights were then put up from neighbourhood of Church and top of AVENUE about U.30.d.40.75. Unfortunately two Lewis guns were out of action, one having a broken striker. One Lewis Gun was sent up from A Coy, but by this time all was quiet. At 22.45 relief of 29th Dn.I. arrived at this bridge.

- 5 -

"Bridge No. 1 was impassable and relief for right Platoon had to take place over No. 2 Bridge.

At 02.30 Nov. 6th relief of Company was reported complete all posts having been handed over intact.

(Sd) J E R Gray.
Capt
O/C B Coy
MEZI

20.30
6-11-18.

CONFIDENTIAL

WAR DIARY

OF

33RD BN. LONDON REGT. (RIFLE BDE.)

FROM 1-12-18   TO 31-12-18

(VOLUME VI.)

[signature]
for Lt. Col.
Commdg. 33rd Bn. London Regt. (RB)

Army Form C. 2118.

WAR DIARY
or
INTELLIGENCE SUMMARY
(Erase heading not required.)

(13)

Place	Date 1918	Hour	Summary of Events and Information	Remarks and references to Appendices
BONDUES	Dec 1		Divine Service. Lieut. G.K.G. BETTANY joined - 30-11-18. Military meals awarded to o/m presented by B.G.C. :-	C.A.M. Sh.
"	2		860472 Rfn. (A/cpl.) C.T. BRADLEY 860607 Rfn. J. OLIVER 860524 " B. FORD 860689 " J. WALKDEN 860521 " J.C. FREEMAN A11450 " W. WIEGMAN Coy. Training & Educational Classes & Relief.	C.A.M. Sh.
"	3		Coy. Training & Educational Classes & Relief.	C.A.M. Sh.
"	4/5		Arm Drill. Close Order Drill. Educational Classes & relief.	C.A.M. Sh.
"	6		A/Cpl. J. McGAVIN GREIG, Messenger on Motor cycle, from M.C. Brigade C. M.S. MATOS C.A.M. VAN MIDDINGEN M.C. despatches. Command. Returned. for Corps Commanders Inspection. Recreation. French Decoration awarded :- CROIX DE GUERRE - Corps (Star) to Lt. Col. J. McGAVIN GREIG CROIX DE GUERRE - Division to 861124 A/C.Q.M.S. ROSS R.S.	C.A.M. Sh.
"	7		Coy. Training. Inspection of Billets by Commanding Officer. Educational Classes.	C.A.M. Sh.
"	8		Divine Service. 2/Lt. J.B. GARDEN. 2/Lt. J.M. PURCHASE joined.	C.A.M. Sh.
"	9		Arm Drill. Close Order Drill & Recreational Games.	C.A.M. Sh.
"	10		Inspection of Division by XV Corps Commander. Recreation.	C.A.M. Sh.
"	11		Battalion moved by Route March to MARCQ. Lt. H.B. MINSHULL joined.	C.A.M. Sh.
MARCQ	12		Cleaning & Improvement of Billets.	C.A.M. Sh.
"	13		Arm Drill - Close Order Drill & Recreational Games.	C.A.M. Sh.
"	14		Distinguished Service Order awarded to T/Capt. J.E.B. GRAY. Military Cross awarded to T/Lt. J.E. OSBORNE. T/Lt. W.D. CASS. T/2/Lt. F.H. FULLER. Distinguished Conduct Medal awarded to :- 860522 Cpl. T. FITZPATRICK - 860417 L/Cpl. A. BARFOOT.	C.A.M. Sh.
"	15		Coy. Training - Inspection of Billets by Commanding Officer.	C.A.M. Sh.
"			Divine Service.	C.A.M. Sh.
"	16/20		Arm Drill. Close Order Drill, Physical Training, Recreational Games, Compulsory Education, Voluntary French Lectures & Classes & Lectures.	C.A.M. Sh.

Army Form C. 2118.

WAR DIARY
or
INTELLIGENCE SUMMARY.
(Erase heading not required.)

Place	Date 1918 Dec	Hour	Summary of Events and Information	Remarks and references to Appendices
MARCQ	21		Coy. Training. Compulsory Education & Recreational Games. Inspection of Billets by Commanding Officer.	Athita
"	22		Divine Service.	Athita
"	23/24		Coy. Training, including P.T. & Compulsory Education. Voluntary Educational Classes & Lectures. Lt.Col. J. McGAVIN CB.E assumed Command of Batn.	Athita
"	25		Christmas Day – Divine Service.	Athita
"	26/27		Coy. Training, including Recreational Games & Compulsory Education. Voluntary Educational Classes & Lectures.	Athita
"	28		— do — — do — Inspection	Athita
"	29		8 Fields by Commanding Officer. Divine Service.	Athita
"	30		Batn. Route March. Voluntary Educational Class.	Athita
"	31		Coy. Training including Compulsory Education & P.T. Voluntary Educational Classes & Lectures. During the month a number of stages were given facilities for attending Lectures at TOURCOING.	Athita

31-12-18.

[signature] Major

for Lt. Col.
Commanding 33rd Bn. London Regt. (Rifle Bde).

CONFIDENTIAL.

WAR DIARY

OF

33rd Bn THE LONDON REGT (RIFLE BDE)

FROM. 1-1-19   To 31-1-19

(VOLUME VII)

(s) M.T. Boscawen Lt Col.
Commdg 33rd Bn The London Regt (Rifle Bde)

31/1/19.

Army Form C. 2118.

WAR DIARY
or
INTELLIGENCE SUMMARY
(Erase heading not required.)

Place	Date 1919	Hour	Summary of Events and Information	Remarks and references to Appendices
MARCQ	JAN. 1st		Capt. S.H. Shoults M.C. rejoined. New Year Dance held for troops & civilians.	
"	2nd		Company training. Compulsory education. Recreational Training.	
"	3rd		Battalion moved to TOURCOING by march route and took over billets from 10th H.L.I.	
TOURCOING	4th		Inspection of billets by Commanding Officer. Coy Training.	
"	5th		Divine Service.	
"	6/9th		Coy Training, Compulsory Education, Recreational Training. A.F.Z. 16 filled in.	
"	10th		Route March.	
"	11th		Inspection of billets by Commanding Officer. Education Lectures & Recreational Training.	
"	12th		Divine Service.	
"	13/16th		Coy Drill, Education, Lectures, Recreational Training.	
"	17th		Battalion route March. Arr. Col. Hon. M.T. Porcaurn D.S.O. M.C. rejoined and assumed Command of Battalion. A/Lt. Col. J. McBain being to 19th Y and here Regt. Rejoined and Inspector of billets by Commanding Officer.	
"	18th		Divine Service.	
"	19th		Coy training, Drill, saluting, guard & education classes, Recreational games.	
"	20/25th		to Hospital 21st Major Card Vin Mellis M.C. assumed command. Inspection of billets by Commanding Officer. Divine Service.	
"	26th		Coy drill, physical training, saluting, guard drill, Recreational P.G. Hon. M.T. Porcaurn D.S.O. M.C. rejoined on 3/1/19 and games, Education and Picture. Arising to work taxation were given to men to attend training lectures. Entertainments were provided and no effort was spared to ensure the comfort and happiness of the troops.	
"	27/30th		5 Officers and 171 Other Ranks were demobilized during the month.	

M.T. Porcaurn Lt Col.
Commd. 3/3 th Loud Regt (Rifle Bde)

CONFIDENTIAL

WAR DIARY

of

33rd Bn The London Regt (Rifle Bde)

From 1-2-19 To 28-2-19

(Volume VIII)

Major
Commdg 33rd Bn London Regt (RB)

Army Form C. 2118.

WAR DIARY
or
INTELLIGENCE SUMMARY

(Erase heading not required.)

Instructions regarding War Diaries and Intelligence Summaries are contained in F. S. Regs., Part II. and the Staff Manual respectively. Title pages will be prepared in manuscript.

(16)

Place	Date 1919	Hour	Summary of Events and Information	Remarks and references to Appendices
TOURCOING	Feb 1st		Physical Training. Arms Drill. Compulsory Education. Inspection of Billets by Commanding Officer	Troops
"	" 2nd		Divine Service	
"	" 3/4		Physical Training. Arms Drill. Recreational Games. Compulsory Education	
"	" 5th		Inspection of Billets by Commanding Officer. 5th and 6th Lecture	
"	" 6/7		Physical Training. Arms Drill. Compulsory Education	
"	" 8th		Divine Service	
"	" 9th			
"	" 10th		Physical Training. Recreational Games. Compulsory Education. Lecture	
"	" 11/12		Arms Drill. Recreational Games. Compulsory Education. Lecture	
"	" 13/14		Physical Training. Arms Drill. Recreational Games. Compulsory Education	
"	" 15th		Inspection of Billets by Commanding Officer. Recreational Games. Compulsory Education	
"	" 16th		Divine Service	
"	" 17/21		Physical Training. Arms Drill. Recreational Games. Compulsory Education	7.2.19 see billets
"	" 22nd		Recreational Games. Physical Training. Compulsory Education. 2.6.C. 2nd Lieut M.T. Brennan M.O. m.c. proceeded on Leave to France. Major S.R.m. Shaw Trollope M.C. assumed command. Inspection of Billets by Commanding Officer	
"	" 23rd		Divine Service	
"	" 24/28		Physical Training. Recreational Games. Compulsory Education. Lecture. During the month numerous Guards + Fatigues for Billets + Journeys were found.	

11 Officers and 304 Other Ranks were demobilised during the month.

Commdg 33rd Bn London Regt (Rifle Bde.)

CONFIDENTIAL

WAR DIARY

— OF —

33RD/1 BN THE LONDON REGT (R.B)

FROM 1/3/19   TO 31/3/19

(VOLUME IX)

_____ Major
Commdg 33rd Bn The London Regt (R.B)

31/3/19.

WAR DIARY
or
INTELLIGENCE SUMMARY

Army Form C. 2118.

Place	Date 1919.	Hour	Summary of Events and Information	Remarks and references to Appendices
TOURCOING.	MARCH 1		Billet Inspection by the Commanding Officer.	
-do-	2		Guard of 1 officer and 67 other Ranks to St André Station.	
-do-	4		Capt J. B. Grant R.S.O. joined Battalion.	Copy
-do-	10		Capt. S. Col. Robinson D.S.O. rejoined Battalion.	
-do-	13		" G. B. McClure	
-do-	"		-do- 14th St André Guard rejoined	Ridley
-do-	16.		Draft of 2/Lt. Z. H. Fuller M.C and 120 Other Ranks proceeded by train from Tourcoing to join 2/17th London Regt - Boulogne.	
-do-	25		Draft of Lt. W. D. Case M.C., Lt E. H. Robinson and 83 Other Ranks proceeded by train from Tourcoing to join 2/23rd London Regt, Calais.	mas-ly-H...
			6 officers and 8 Other Ranks were demobilised during the month. 20 other Ranks re-enlisted and dispatched to U.K. on final leave. Practically all available men having been utilised for various Guards at St André & Tourcoing Stations and Ammunition Dumps, very little, if any Training was carried out during the month.	
-do-	29		Lt Col. Hon M. T. Boscawen D.S.O., M.C. proceeded to join 2/16th London Regt., and Major C. A. M. Van Millingen M.C., assumed Command of the Battalion.	

C.A.M. Van Millingen
Major
Commdg 3/7th The London Regt (Rifle Bde).

CONFIDENTIAL

WAR DIARY OF

33ʳᴰ Bⁿ THE LONDON REGT (R.B)

PERIOD 1-4-19 to 30-4-19.

(VOLUME X)

Shovellor Capt a/Adjt for Major
———————————————— Commanding
33rd Bn. The London Regt. (Rifle Brigade).

1/5/19

Army Form C. 2118.

WAR DIARY
or
INTELLIGENCE SUMMARY.
(Erase heading not required.)

Instructions regarding War Diaries and Intelligence Summaries are contained in F. S. Regs., Part II. and the Staff Manual respectively. Title pages will be prepared in manuscript.

Place	Date 1919	Hour	Summary of Events and Information	Remarks and references to Appendices
TOURCOING	Apr 2nd		Capt J. Blake and details of 14th M.G. Batt. attached to Batt. for administration purposes.	
"	19th		14th M.G. Details (34 other ranks) proceeded to join 62nd M.G. Batt.	

Mulneley Capt & Adjt for Major
Commanding
33rd Bn. The London Regt. (Rifle Brigade).

CONFIDENTIAL.

WAR DIARY OF

33rd Battn. The London Regiment (Rifle Bde)

From 1.5.1919 To 31.5.1919.

(VOLUME XI)

[signature], Major.
Commdg. 33rd Bn. The London Regt. (R.B.)

Army Form C. 2118.

WAR DIARY
or
INTELLIGENCE SUMMARY

(Erase heading not required.)

Place	Date 1919	Hour	Summary of Events and Information	Remarks and references to Appendices
TOURCOING.	MAY 13		Capt. A.E.H. ROBINSON D.S.O. proceeded to report to 313 P. of W. Coy for duty.	
do.	17		/Lt. H.R. PATSTON M.M. " " " 328 " "	
do.	20		Capt. WENHAM proceeded to report to British Mission BERLIN.	
do.	20		Capt. J.E.B. GRAY D.S.O. left England to report to British Mission BERLIN.	
do.	31		One Officer and 8 other Ranks were demobilized during the month.	

MAJOR.
Commanding
33rd Bn. The London Regt. (Rifle Brigade).

www.ingramcontent.com/pod-product-compliance
Lightning Source LLC
Chambersburg PA
CBHW081456160426
43193CB00013B/2500